D0570536

CHARMING WUSHAN

Nov. 1st, 2011

魅力巫山

宋开平

Marc + Barb

Great Trip to the

Lesser Three Gorges

海南出版社
Hainan Publishing House

Song Peiping

目錄

Contents

魅力巫山

序

一位從未到過長江三峽的朋友曾經告訴我：很多年以來，在他的潛意識裏，三峽是籠罩在一片輕紗薄霧之中的，一如沙漠中的海市蜃樓一般，可隱隱望到，但遙不可及。可見，在人們心裏，三峽是美麗而又神秘的。她占盡了山的雄渾、水的靈動；她孕育過204萬年前的人類始祖，擁有着輝煌燦爛的大溪文明；她有屈原、昭君這樣的優秀兒女，留下過李白、杜甫、白居易走過的腳印；她擁有着太多美麗的傳說，有大禹的堅韌神女的柔美。她是一幅畫、一首詩、一本書、一個夢……

千百年來，無數文人墨客都在用自己的方式解讀三峽。在這裏，屈原抒發的是憂國憂民的博大胸襟，宋玉編織着纏綿悱惻的動人傳說，李白激發出恣肆汪洋的浪漫情懷，毛澤東譜寫了氣壯山河的豪邁詩篇……在現實中，三峽是唯一的，世界祇有一個三峽。而在人們的心裏，三峽又都是不同的，每一個人的心裏都有一個屬于自己的三峽。

大約是從上世紀70年代起，有這麼一群三峽人開始以新的方式解讀他們眼裏的三峽，那就是攝影。在那個年代，對于三峽這個相對還很偏僻和落後的地方，即便是一臺普通得不能再普通的海鷗120相機，也是非常奢侈和不可想象的。人們對這種新式的精密儀器有着莫名的敬畏，對挎上相機的這群三峽人自然也是非常的尊崇。因爲他們可以把家鄉的一山一水都變成"畫"，印在各種各樣的書上，讓天南地北的人都可以看到。通過他們的眼睛，世界認識了三峽。

本書作者宋開平先生就是其中的一位。這個地地道道的三峽漢子，當過教師，放過電影，幹過美工，做過政府官員，也出任過企業老總。幾十年來，他把幾乎所有的業餘時間都奉獻給了三峽，奉獻給了攝影。象苦行僧一般，他默默地行走在峽江之間，用快門解讀三峽，也解讀自己的人生。無數次忍饑挨餓，無數次日曬雨淋，無數次命懸一綫，換回的是數以萬計的優秀攝影作品。他把青春和生命交給了三峽，把自己熔入了這片土地。或者說，他已經是三峽的一部分了。

在宋開平先生的眼裏，三峽是神聖的，所以他才會用那樣虔誠的心去貼近它；三峽是唯美的，所以他才會那樣苛刻地對待自己的每一次創作；三峽是鮮活的，所以他的作品才有了那樣強大的生命力；三峽是多元的，所以在他才會從那麼豐富的層面去解讀三峽。欣賞宋開平先生的攝影作品，你可以領略三峽的無限風光，品味三峽的民風民俗、了解三峽的滄桑變化，感受三峽的人文精神。在光影的世界裏，他觸摸到的是三峽的靈魂。

"雄關漫道真如鐵，而今邁步從頭越"。今天，我們更欣喜地看到，退休後的宋開平先生沒有停下求索的腳步，他已經站在一個新的起跑綫上，以更加澎湃的激情，更加理性的思考、更加獨特的視角、更加新穎的手法在解讀三峽。我們相信也倍加期待他能創作出更多更優秀的作品。

是爲序。

江　上
2007年7月于渝州

Preface

Once a friend of mine who has never been to the Yangtze Three Gorges, told me a beautiful story about these gorges. In his mind, the Yangtze Three Gorges appear like this-they are just covered by changeable mists. They could be seen but could not be reached, just like a mirage in the desert. Hence, the Three Gorges are beautiful and mysterious. It combines huge mountains with soft water. In Wushan,more than 2.04-million-year-old Wushan Ape-men and the Daxi Culture were discovered. The talented Quyuan and pretty Zhaojun were born here. The famous poets, such as Libai, Dufu, and Bai Juyi also set foot here. There are many fairy tales about these mountains and rivers. The Three Gorges are like a painting, a poem, a book, a dream.

Many poets and men of literature have tried hard to understand more about the Three Gorges with their own thoughts over the centuries. For example, Quyuan has become a concerned patriot, Songyu has become a sentimental king and Libai a romantic poet. Even chairman Mao Cedong has composed lots of inspiring and uplifting poems. In fact, the Three Gorges are unique in the world. Yet, everyone has his own Three Gorges in his heart.

In the 1970's, a group of native photographers used another way to learn about the Three Gorges through picture-taking. At that time, this area was quite remote and backward. Even a very ordinary Seagulf Brand Camera 120 was a luxury. For the local people, it was a mysterious and an unimaginable thing.And these photographers were respected here and there, because they could use their own cameras to capture their hometown's beautiful mountain and river scenery. Now, other people from around the world can also know and understand the Three Gorges much better by looking at their wonderful pictures being published inside many books.

Song kaiping, one of these local photographers, is the photographer of this picture book. He is the very essence of the Three Gorges man. He used to be a teacher, a movie man, a painter, a government official as well as a general manager in a company. He has dedicated all his spare time to the Three Gorges and his photography career. He works alone around the Three Gorges, using the camera to study the three Gorges and his own life. He has taken many fantastic pictures during his hard work. Many times. he went hungry, encountered terrible weather, and once almost lost his life. He loves the Three Gorges very much and has totally dedicated his youth and life into it. In one word, he is part of the Three Gorges.

In Mr. Song's eyes, the Three Gorges are divine. The Three Gorges are close to his heart. To him the Three Gorges are pure beauty and alive. He is very disciplined with his picture-taking. His masterpieces are very much appreciated.The Three Gorges are multi-faceted. He can understand them from many perspectives.From Mr. Song's photography, you may enjoy the Three Gorges' beautiful scenery, taste its rich folk customs, understand its great changes, and feel its people's spirits. What he has touched is the soul of the Three Gorges through his photography.

Today, we are very glad to know that the retired Mr. Song still continues to work hard on his photography career. Standing on a new starting line, he would like to learn and understand more about the Three Gorges with his passion, thoughts, unique perspectives and latest methods. We are looking forward to his outstanding pictures in the near future.

The above is the preface. It was written by Jiangshan in July 2007 in Chongqing .

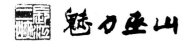

巫山

《中國古今地名大辭典》載：巫山，是巴山山脈突起之處。今南陵山上，綿延的山頂和山腳的大江以及中間的一道大山梁直插江岸，形成"工"字，兩旁縱橫的溝壑形成兩個"人"字，各排一邊，組合起來，恰似一個"巫"字，在這"巫"字的西邊，三道山梁垂直山腳，酷是"山"字。縣境內有長江三峽之巫峽、十二峰、神女溪、巫山小三峽、小小三峽、大昌古鎮、梨子坪森林公園及距今204萬年"巫山人博物館"、"大溪文化遺址"等著名的國家級風景名勝區和人文景觀。

巫山縣城，小巧優雅，十二條街道用巫峽十二峰命名，占地不到一平方公裏，古代青石城牆、東南西北四個城門一直保存到縣城拆遷。縣城歷史悠久，早在二千多年前即初具規模。三峽大壩修建後，巫山縣城于2002年12月全部拆遷完畢。2003年6月10日晚，三峽水庫蓄水135米，巫山老縣城全部淹沒，時年2280歲。

新縣城占地5平方公裏，是老縣城的5倍有餘，主幹道廣東路長3.6公裏，寬32米，橫貫東西。神女大道寬30米，縱向自平湖路直上，穿越主幹道，形成城市的主軸綫。其餘縱橫交錯且有地方特色的淨壇路、翠屏路、集仙路等十餘條街道長達30于公裏。新縣城"一路一燈一景，一街一樹一花，"每條街道的路燈樣式，行道樹的品種各成風姿，各具美色。如夜，華燈綻放，倒映平湖，在巫山群峰的懷抱裏，分外妖嬈，巫山贏得了"中國優秀旅游城區"、"國家衛生城區"、"國家生態示範區"等光榮稱號。

巫山移民新縣城 New Wushan Immigration County Seat

Wushan

Wushan is at the top of Mt. Bashan. It is named Wushan because overlooking Wushan city, Mt. Naling looks like the Chinese characters "Wu" and "Shan" seen from afar.

The beautiful and tiny ancient Wushan Town covers an area of less than one square kilometer, with 12 streets named after the 12 peaks inside the Wu Gorge. Before the whole town was demolished, the four ancient town gates could still be seen. The town can be traced back more than 2000 years ago. With the building of the Yangtze Three Gorges Project, the town was totally destroyed and demolished in 2002. In June, 2003, the whole town was submerged with the water level reaching 135 meters on the Yangtze River. The town ended its 2280-year-old history.

The new Wushan city covers an area of 5 square kilometers and is 5 times larger than the old one. The main Guangdong Road is 3.6 km long and 32 meters wide. The Goddess Road is the city's main road. The total length of the roads in the city reach over 30 km. Each road has its own kind of lamps, flowers, trees and views. The night views of Wushan become more and more attractive with colorful neon lights. Now Wushan has won the title of "China's Best Tourist Attraction", "National Level Civilized City" and "State Ecological Model Area".

高峡平湖巫山秀　beautiful Wushan With high gorge and smooth lake

小三峡秋色　autumn in the Lesser Three Gorges

無限秀美處，最是小三峽 the most beautiful Lesser Three Gorges

巫峡烟云 mists and clouds in Wu Gorge

巫峽

　　在長江三峽中，巫峽以幽深秀麗而聞名，它西起巫山縣的大寧河與長江的匯合處，東至巴東縣的官渡口，全長46公裏。巫峽境內，群山環繞，溝壑縱橫，山青水碧，名峰爭秀，尤以"十二峰"引人入勝。十二峰是以其山峰的自然形態，分別賦予形象化的美名。巫峽南北兩岸各有六峰，北岸是登龍峰、聖泉峰、朝雲峰、神女峰、鬆巒峰、集仙峰；南岸是翠屏峰、聚鶴峰、飛鳳峰、起雲峰、上升峰、淨壇峰。三峽大壩156水位後，神女峰下非常幽深秀麗、原始生態的"神女溪風景區"，得到了充分的開發利用，是三峽難得的一新辟風景區。

Wu Gorge

　　The Wu Gorge extends eastward from the mouth of the Daning River in the east of Wushan County to Guandukou in Badong County, with a length of 45 kilometers. The Wu Gorge is characterized by beautiful peaks and steep cliffs on either side. "Sailing downstream to Wu Gorge, I have my heart only in the twelve peaks of Mt. Wushan." The twelve peaks of Mt. Wushan stand on both sides of the gorge. On the north there are six peaks-Denglong(Soaring Dragon), Shengquan(Holy. Spring), Chaoyun(To-the-Cloud), Shennu(Fairy), Songluan(Pines), Jixian(Fairy-Gathering), and on the south another.. six-Juhe(Flock-of-Cranes), Cuiping(Green Screen), Feifeng(Flying Phoenix), and Shangsheng(Ascent). All these well-known scenic spots face the green water and offer ever-lasting charms.

神女峰 Shennu Peak

14

魅力巫山

巫峡夕照 sunset in Wu Gorge

巫峡出口处　exit of Wu Gorge

林蔭巫峡　forest shelter in Wu Gorge

黄金水道 golden water course

一覧巫峽諸峰 overlooking peaks in Wu Gorge

1.淨壇峰　Jingtan Peak　　2.集仙峰　Jixian Peak
3.聖泉峰　Shengquan Peak　4.神女峰　Shennu Peak

巫峡雪景 snow in Wu Gorge

魅力巫山

巫峡之春 spring in Wu Gorge

舟行巫峽彩雲間 boats sailing in colourful Wu Gorge

寧河長江交匯處 the conflunence of the Yangtze River and Daning River

鳥瞰巫峽 bird's eye view of Wu Gorge

峽谷畫廊 picturesque valley

巫峡秋色 autumn in Wu Gorge

峡江峭壁 steep cliffs in the gorge

大江东去 great river flowing eastward

神女溪

　　與神女峰一江之隔的神女溪，是高峽平湖後新開發的一景區，峽谷兩岸峭壁參天，藤蔓懸挂，一江碧水，十分幽靜，保留了三峽原始狀態之美，是一處難得的美如盆景的新景區。巫山十二峰中的上升峰、起雲峰、淨壇峰就在神女溪內。

Goddess Brook

　　The Goddess Brook is on the opposite of the Goddess Peak. It is a newly developed tourist scenic area. It remains largely unspoiled. Though short and small, the scenery inside is marvelous, secluded and primitive. The views of Jingtan, Qiyun and Shangsheng Peaks can be totally enjoyed along the Goddess Brook.

碧波蕩舟
boating on the rippling blue waves

峭壁畫廊 picturesque sheer cliffs

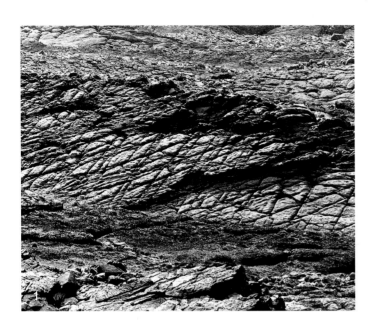

1.2.3.4.5.6.7.千姿百态的三峡石 unique three gorges rock

1.2.3.千姿百態的三峡石　unique three gorges rock
4.5.三峡縴夫石　rocks cut by tracker ropes

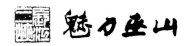

巫山小三峡

　　巫山小三峡，國家級風景名勝區，中國旅游勝地四十佳，中國首批AAAAA級旅游風景區，被譽爲"中華奇觀"、"天下絕景"。

　　巫山小三峡所在的大寧河，是三峡段最大的一條支流，發源于渝、陝、鄂交界的大巴山南麓，由北向南，在巫峽口注入長江。

　　巫山小三峡是大寧河流經巫山境內的龍門峽、巴霧峽、滴翠峽三段峽谷的總稱。景區內有多姿多彩的奇峰峻嶺，變幻無窮的激流險灘，清幽秀潔的飛瀑清泉，千姿百態的倒懸鐘乳，神秘莫測的懸崖古洞，栩栩如生的自然雕塑，茂密繁盛的山林竹木，是一處玲瓏奇巧的天然盆景；有千餘衹頑皮猴群、數百衹情侶鴛鴦、數十種奇异水鳥和魚類，是一處絕妙的動物王國；有迷存千古的巴人懸棺、船棺，是一處珍貴的歷史遺迹。

Lesser Three Gorges in Wushan

The Lesser Three Gorges In Wushan, regarded as "China Wonder" and "Unmatched Landscape in the world", is at the national level of tourists' attractions, being the top forty tourist attraction in China, and being the first AAAAA tourist scenic area in China.

The Daning River inside the Lesser Three Gorges, is the biggest tributary in the Yangtze Three Gorges region. It takes its source from the sourthern slope of Mt. Daba in the boundary of Chongqing City, Shanxi and Hubei Provinces, pouring itself into the Yangtze at the western entrance to the Wu Gorge from north to south.

The Lesser Three Gorges in Wushan consists of three separate parts, called "Dragon-Gate Gorge", "Misty Gorge" and "Emerald Gorge". It is characterized by its unique sights, surrounded by green mountains and clear water along both sides of the river, with towering peaks, strange cliffs and simple mysteries of nature. Inside the gorges, birds' song and monkeys' chatter can sometimes be heard from both banks. Tourists can see a thousand-year-old suspended coffin, the mandarin ducks dancing on the crystal river, the stalactites in various shapes and charming cliffside springs and waterfalls.

綠水青山小三峡 beautiful water and green mountain in the Lesser Three Gorges

翠谷輕舟 sailing boats in the emerald valley

龍門峽

龍門峽是小三峽的第一峽，從峽口至東坪壩全長10公裏，是小三峽中最短的一個峽。峽內絕壁對峙，高峽束江，天開一綫，形若一門。素有"不是夔門，勝似夔門"、"雄哉，龍門峽"之稱。

Dragon Gate Gorge

Dragon Gate Gorge, 10km long, is the first and shortest gorge of the three. The cliffs on either side form a natural gate, magnificent and spectacular. As it resembles "Kuimen", the gorge is also known as the "Small Kuimen".

追波逐浪 boating by waves

新龍門大橋 new Dragon-Gate Bridge

駛進小三峽　going into the Lesser Three Gorges

昔日龍門大橋　former Dragon-Gate Bridge

1.青獅守門　gate guarded by lion
2.靈芝峰　fungus Peak
3.逝去的"銀窩灘"　flooded Yinwo Rapids

魅力巫山

巴霧峽

Misty Gorge

巴霧峽是小三峽的第二個峽，全長15公裏，峽內山高谷深，雲霧迷蒙，鐘乳密布，千奇萬狀，怪石嶙峋，峰回路轉，水盡疑無路，拐彎別有天。素有"奇哉，巴霧峽"之贊。

Misty Gorge, 15km long, is the second gorge. Inside the gorge, the towering peaks with a deep valley, changeable mists, and various stalactites can be seen everywhere.

仙桃峰 Fairy Peach Peak

巴霧晨渡 morning ferry in Misty Gorge

蓮臺峰 Lotus Platform Peak

小三峡鐘乳 Stalactites in the Lesser Three Gorges

1.巴霧奇崖　unique rocks in Misty Gorge
2.八仙拜觀音　Piggy Worshipping Mercy of Goddess
3.昔日"馬歸山"　flooded Horse Returning into Mountain

漫山紅葉似彩霞 mountains covered by reddish leaves

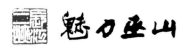

滴翠峽

　　滴翠峽是小三峽的第三個峽，全長
25公裏，這裏是小三峽最幽深、最秀麗的
一個峽谷。兩岸無處不蒼翠，有水盡飛
花。峽中流泉飛瀑，淙淙有聲，秀洞奇
崖，絢麗多姿，石寨高築，古色古香，猴
群攀援，猿聲陣陣，饒有野趣。素有"幽
哉，滴翠峽"之譽。

Emerald Gorge

　　The Emerald Gorge, 25 km long, is the
third gorge. It is the most secluded and
beautiful gorge among the three. Green
mountains, green water, and green bamboos
can be seen everywhere. The beautiful
waterfalls splash into the river on either side
of the mountain. An ancient Buddha Temple
sits almost half way up the mountain. The
wild monkeys can be found jumping from
branch to branch. How secluded the Emerald
Gorge is!

滴翠峽 Emerald Gorge

天泉飛雨 heaven-sent spring like dancing rain

幽谷翠竹 green bamboos in secluded gorge

鐘乳聽濤 waves kissing stalactites

碧水泛舟 boating on the green water

1.飛雲洞 Flying Clouds Cave
2.羅家寨 the Lou's Stockaded Village

3.群仙迎賓 rock statue welcoming guests
4.雙鷹戲屏 two rock eagles playing on the screen

1.大宁盐泉　a brine factory along Daning River
2.古栈道遗址　ruins of ancient plank walkway
3.赤壁摩天 grand sky-high bronze precipice

滴翠峡 Emerald Gorge

新仿古栈道　new imitation plank walkway

新型觀光游船　traditional chinese style tourist boat

紅葉漫山 reddish leaves on the mountain

魅力巫山

又是漫山紅葉時 reddish leaves covering mountains again

又是漫山紅葉時 reddish leaves covering mountains again

小三峡野生動物 wild animals in the Lesser Three Gorges

小三峡野生植物　wild plants in the Lesser Three Gorges

魅力巫山

小小三峽

　　小小三峽是三撑峽、秦王峽、長灘峽的總稱。風景氣勢磅礴，峽幽、景奇、瀑布多姿。

　　小小三峽兩岸山峰，和小三峽的山峰海拔高度一樣，而河道狹窄。三撑峽中，河道窄處，祇有撑船的蒿杆長度，連綿數裏。人坐船中，岸壁伸手可觸。植被原始，古藤、怪石、秀峰奇岩，飄逸多姿的山水畫卷。美妙的傳說，給小小三峽增添神韵。

　　小小三峽，養在深閨人已知，高峽平湖的小小三峽，既有平湖碧波的魅力，又有急流險灘，是對小三峽淹沒後沒了險灘、急流的補償。泛舟其間，別有一番情趣。

Mini Three Gorges

　　The Mini-three Gorges, consists of the Changtan Gorge, Qingwang Gorge and Sancheng Gorge. It features its secluded valley, magniflcent cliffs, flying waterfalls and rare stalactites. Ancient vines hang down from the cliffs and colorful wildflowers bloom. The Madu River goes through narrow valleys. Inside the gorge, the greenish water is so peaceful that you can soothe the soul.

　　The opening of the Mini-three Gorges provides you to enjoy the calm lake like river as well as wild and scenic rivers with currents and rapids. It remains fresh and healthy with nature.

泛舟探幽 seeking seclusion by boating

穿梭歡舟 boats coming and going

推船過灘 pulling boats against rapids

小三峡纤夫 boat trackers in the Lesser Three Gorges

堆綠叠翠 pretty emerald

漂游覓樂　having fun by white-water rafting

漂游覓樂　having fun by white-water rafting

小小三峡纤夫　boat trackers in the Mini Three Gorges

小小三峡纤夫 boat trackers in the Mini Three Gorges

懸棺

　　小三峽的龍門峽、巴霧峽、滴翠峽中的懸崖峭壁上都有懸棺。龍門峽的懸棺在文化大革命中已遭破壞，不復存在了。在巴霧峽、滴翠峽離河面四五百米高懸崖的洞穴上都有巴人懸棺。千百年來，風吹雨蝕，人事滄桑，懸棺之謎，眾說紛紜。民謠說："紅崖對白崖，金銀滿棺材，捨得兒和女，走攏就拿來。"據考古工作者研究，懸棺是戰國時代居住在這一帶的濮族人的葬棺。從棺中主葬者和殉葬品銅帶鈎、銅手鐲等判斷，它距今已有2000多年的歷史。據唐代張鷟考證：在古代，父母死後，子女"盡產爲棺，于臨江高山半肋鑿龕以葬之，自山上懸索下柩，彌高者以爲至孝。"

Suspending Coffin

　　The suspending coffins can be seen inside the Lesser Three Gorges. The coffin inside the "Dragon-Gate Gorge" was destroyed during the Cultural Revolution in the 1960's. In the "Misty Gorge" and "Emerald Gorge", over 2,000-year-old "hanging" coffin can be seen suspended on a precipices high up on the cliff-face. So far, there is no good and quick answer to the mysterious hanging coffin. From the archaeologists, the hanging coffin can be dated back more than 2,000 years ago. It belonged to the minority Ba people. They lowered the wooden coffin from the top of the mountain. The higher they put the coffin on the cliff, the higher the social status they had !

荆竹壩懸棺群 cliff coffins in JinZhuba

飛雲洞懸棺 cliff coffin in Flying Cloud Cave

小三峽船棺 boat coffin in Lesser Three Gorges

巴霧峽懸棺 cliff coffin in Misty Gorge

滴翠峽懸棺 cliff coffin in Emerald Gorge

大昌古鎮

大昌古鎮很小，被人們稱爲"袖珍古城"。城內屋宇多屬明清兩代建築，雕梁畫棟，精巧別致。大昌古鎮現已整體搬遷，原樣恢復明清一條街。新街與古鎮，交相輝映，湖光山色，更具魅力。

Ancient Dachang Town

The ancient Dachang Town receives its reputation as the "Mini Ancient Town" because it is so tiny in size. The architecture of most of the buildings and houses are of the Ming or Qing Dynasty style. Now the whole ancient Dachang Town has been removed. One of the streets was rebuilt, remaining the same style as in Ming and Qing Dynasty. It is most attractive and enjoyable for tourists.

古城南門 southern gate in ancient town

原樣復建的大昌移民新鎮 reproduced new immig ration Dachang Town

古鎮一角 a corner in ancient town

古鎮一角 a corner in ancient town

民間節日 local folk festival

古鎮風情 folk customs in ancient town

魅力巫山

梨子坪森林公園

梨子坪森林公園與小三峽國家森林公園相鄰，距縣城45公裏，總面積1，383公頃，平均海拔1，800米，年平均氣溫18.4攝氏度，森林覆蓋率達95%以上，是鑲嵌在大小三峽之間第一顆綠色明珠。

Li Ziping Forest Park

The Li Ziping Forest Park is very close to the national Lesser Three Gorges Park. It is 45km from the Wushan County seat. It covers an area of 1,383 hectares with an average height of 1,800 meters above sea level and an average annual temperature of 18.4. The forest coverage is more than 95 percent. It is the first green forest pearl between the Yangtze Three Gorges and the Lesser Three Gorges.

秋色 autumn scenery

冬景 winter view

相思水 lovesickness water

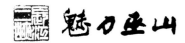

巫山風情

考古發現，早在204萬年前，就有人類在巫山生活，亞洲人類從這裏起步！被考古學家稱爲"巫山人"；

在四五千年前的新石器時期，小三峽的琵琶洲一帶，開始有大量的巫山人在那裏勞動、生習、繁衍了；

兩千多年前，勤勞聰明的巫山人從龍門峽口至飛雲洞百餘裏的懸崖峭壁上，修鑿了一條傳爲我國最長的古棧道，其孔間距離均勻，方孔的大小、深度一致，空孔的排列與河面平行。不難想象，在當時生產力極其低下的條件下，能修出如此壯觀的歷史奇迹，這是多麼的不容易，這正是巫山人聰明才智的結晶。

同是兩千多年前，小三峽懸崖峭壁的懸棺，爲何葬那麼高？如何放上去的？衆說紛紜，專門工作者研究多年，也未得出定論。這不難說明，富有聰明才智的巫山人，在兩千多年前辦到的事，時到今日，其後代還在研究，探討之中，以揭開此迷。

巫山人勤勞、樸實、憨厚、聰明！

今日，巫山人的數十代傳人，正在抓住三峽工程建成後"高峽出平湖"的有利契機，發揮他們的聰明才智，把自己的家鄉建成生態、環保、文明、富足的國際旅游景區！

Industrious Wushan People

From what the archaeologists found, people began to live and prosper in Wushan more than 2.04 million years ago. The archaeologists named them as "Wushan People".

In the New Stone Age period, about 5,000 years ago, there was a large number of Wushan people labouring, working and prospering around the Pipazhou area inside the Lesser Three Gorges.

More than 2,000 years ago, the industrious Wushan people built the longest ancient plank walkway on the cliff along the Daning River. So far, no good answers can explain how people could build the same square holes with such primitive tools. It really is a miracle!

Also, people still have no good answers about the 2,000-year old suspending coffins. For example, we do not know how and why they put the coffin so high on the cliff. Everybody just has his own ideas. It is still a mystery for all of us. Nowadays, We have some experts trying to find the answer about the hanging coffins.

How industrious, smart, simple and honest the Wushan people are!

Today, the descendants of Wushan people are taking the opportunity of completing the Yangtze Three Gorges Project to build their hometown into a ecological, environmental, civilized and wealthy international tourist area.

舞龍 dragon-dancing

舞獅 lion-dancing

舞船 boat-dancing

龍舟競渡 dragon-boat racing

天主教堂 catholic church

1.2.3.三峽農民喜迎親
farmers welcome bride happily in the three gorges

喜收玉米 corn-harvesting

1.高架面 high shelf noodles　　2.做瓦 making tile
3.做布鞋 making cloth shoes　　4.磨面　griding for the corn powder

魅力巫山

賣糧 selling grains

磨刀 sickle-sharpening

開心老漢 happy old man

蓑草打包 sedge grass packing

造木船 making wooden boat

編竹棚 weaving bamboo shed

自制草紙 home-made paper

三峽農夫 farmers in the Three Gorges

赶集 going to the fair

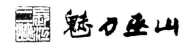

巫山民居

　　生長在三峽地區的巫山人，根據當地的地理條件和氣候環境，就地取材創造了獨具特色的巫山民居。

　　民居以四合院爲多，當地人俗稱"天井"，天井數量的多少，成爲衡量規格的代名詞，建築材料以木頭、靑磚爲主，工藝較爲精致。

　　小場鎮民居并列形成街道，沿街都設有較寬的檐廊，它旣可保護牆體，檐下還可遮陽避雨、擺攤經商。并采用前店後宅、上店下宅的形式，滿足多功能之需要。

　　鄉村民居更是因地制宜、就地取材，除土木結構的四合天井院外，更多則利用黃土、石頭、草梗、石板等材料，建成土牆草屋、石牆石屋，旣省錢又實用，別有一番風情。

Wushan Folk House

　　The native Wushan people living in the Yangtze Three Gorges area have created their unique Wushan style houses according to the local geographical and climate conditions.

　　The majority of the houses are known as the "courtyard", nicknamed as "heavenly well" by native people because of the shapes of the houses. The greater number of houses around the heavenly well shows the people are richer. The building materials for the houses are mainly wood and bricks with richly decorated arts and crafts.

　　The arrangement of small town houses standing side by side form the street. Along the street the eaves protect the house wall. Under the eaves the place can be used for weather shelter as well as opening business stores. Usually the house is arranged in two ways. One is a shop in the front of the house, the other is a shop on the second floor of the house. By such arrangements, it can meet all kinds of needs.

　　Rural houses were built in line with local conditions and materials. With the exception of civil engineering structure courtyard houses, the earth, rock, grass, and the flagstone were used for building country cottages and stone houses. In this way, the local people could save much money. It is also very practical to build such Wushan style house. Come and visit, and you will have a wonderful experience!

四合院 courtyard

巫山老縣城 former Wushan County

江邊民居 riverside folk houses

石板屋 slit house

木板屋 wooden plank house

石头墙 rocked wall

古城門 ancient town gate

石板小街 flagging street

鄉村小鎮 village township

三峡移民

　　移民是三峡工程成败的关键，党中央和国务院非常重视三峡移民工程。受国务院的指派，全国21个省、市、自治区和50多个国家机关对口支援三峡库区，有力地促进了三峡库区的移民安置工作。从2000年到2009年前夕，113万移民分4期迁移安置，到2006年为止，三峡库区按国家计划完成了三斯移民安置任务。库区移民舍小家顾大家，支持三峡工程为国家，依依离别故土，搬迁到了新的家园，开始了新的生活、学习和劳作。

　　The focus of the Yangtze Three Gorges Project is how to relocate the people there successfully. And the Chinese government attaches great importance to the immigration issue. Under the leadership of the State Consul, 21 provinces, municipalities and autonomous regions as well as over 50 state government departments were asked to help them to move away. It is proved that this is quite a good success. From the year 2,000 to 2,009, 1.13 million people will be removed in four stages. Up to the year 2,006, the former three stages have already finished successfully according to the project scheldule. In order to support the Yangtze Three Gorges Project, the immigrants give up their own land to move away. They really have sacrificed a lot and have moved to their new homeland with a totally better new life.

長江三峽

　　長江三峽是瞿塘峽、巫峽、西陵峽的總稱，西起重慶市奉節縣的白帝城，東到宜昌市的南津關，全長193公裏。它是長江風光中的精華，神州山水中的瑰寶，古往今來，閃耀着迷人的光彩，無數中外游客爲之顛倒。整個三峽，兩岸群山壁立，峭壁危崖，峽谷中，斷壁千仞，一水中流，水爲峽束，幽深險峭。長江三峽都以群峰對峙，峭壁嵯峨著稱，各具特色：瞿塘峽最爲雄偉險峻，巫峽以幽深秀麗聞名，西陵峽以灘多水急著稱。峽谷地形封閉，濕氣蒸鬱難散，極易成雲致雨，又以巫山烟雲最負盛名，古人曾贊譽："曾經滄海難爲水，除卻巫山不是雲"。三峽，是中國十大風景名勝區，中國旅游勝地四十佳之一。

Yangtze Three Gorges

　　The Yangtze Three Gorges extends from White King Town in Fengjie County, Chongqing City to Nanjingguan Pass in Yichang City, Consisting of Qutang Gorge, Wu Gorge and Xiling Gorge, with a full length of 193km. It gets the essence of the scenery on the Yangtze River. As a unique landscape of China, it has been displaying its special charm for thousands of years. Inside the gorge region, the peaks tower into the sky, the steep cliffs face one another, and the jagged rocks are of grotesque shapes. The Qutang Gorge is magnificent, the Wu Gorge is elegant, and the Xiling Gorge is perilous. The unique climate of the gorge region produces rare scenes of different weather. The rain and clouds of Mt. Wushan are very changeable and colourful. In other words, the change is unpredictable just as it is described in an ancient poem: "Having been to a vast sea, one will never think much of the water in a river, and one will find no clouds attractive comparing them with those of the Wushan Mountain".

　　The Yangtze Gorges are one of the ten most famous scenic sites of China and is the top forty tourist attractions of China .

鳥瞰三峽
a bird's eye view on the Three Gorges

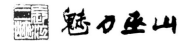

瞿塘峽

順江而下，首先進入三峽中以"雄"著稱的瞿塘峽，瞿塘峽東起巫山縣大溪鄉，西到奉節白帝城，峽長雖然祇有8公裏，是三峽中最短的一個峽，卻有"西控巴蜀收萬壑，東連荊楚壓群山"的雄偉氣勢，是一幅神奇的自然畫卷和文化藝術走廊。峽中可見粉壁牆、倒掉和尚、孟良梯、鳳凰飲泉、風箱峽以及夔門等景觀。

Qutang Gorge

The Qutang Gorge, the most magnificent and shortest one among the Yangtze Three Gorges, extends eastward from White King Town to Daxi Town. Although the gorge is no more than eight kilometers long, it has the capability of controlling the water from Sichuan in the west and dominating the mountains of Hubei in the east. Qutang Gorge boasts not only splendid sights but also places of historical interest, such as the White Washed Wall, Meng Liang Ladder, Monk Hung Upside-Down, FengXiang Crevices and the Magnificence of Kuimen.

瞿塘峽秋韵 The Autumn in Qutang Gorge

鎖江鐵柱 iron pilliar river-lock

赤甲樓 chijia ancient building

瞿塘峡 Qutang Gorge

魅力巫山

燈影樓 Latern Shadow Gorge

西陵春色 spring in Xiling Gorge

西陵峽

　　西陵峽，西起秭歸縣香溪河口，東至宜昌市南津關，全長76公裏，是長江三峽最長的峽谷，因位於夷陵（宜昌古稱）西邊，故名西陵峽。西陵峽以險出名，以奇著稱，西陵峽中有"三灘"（泄灘、青灘、崆嶺灘）、"四峽"（燈影峽、黃牛峽、牛肝馬肺峽和兵書寶劍峽），峽中有峽，灘中有灘，自古三峽船夫世世代代在此與險灘急流相博。葛洲壩工程建成蓄水，回水百裏，險灘變坦途了。

Xiling Gorge

　　The Xiling Gorge stretches 76km from the mouth of Xiangxi River in Zigui County in the west to the Nanjingguan Pass in Yichang city in the east. Xiling Gorge was well-known for its danger because of its large number of shoals and torrents. The three most dangerous shoals are Qingtan Shoal, Xietan Shoal and Kongling shoal. In Xiling Gorge lie four small Gorges-Tactics Books and Sword, Bull's Liver and Horse's Lung, Shadow Play, and the Ox Gorge. All along Xiling there are gorges upon gorges and shoals upon shoals.In the past, the boat trackers struggled with shoals and currents from generation to generation. With the building of Ge Zhouba Dam, navigation has been made possible.

晨過西陵 morning in Xiling Gorge

魅力巫山

重慶市

重慶，長江上游的一顆璀璨明珠。1997年6月（全國人大通過重慶直轄時間爲1997年3月14日，重慶直轄市挂牌爲1997年6月18日。）設爲中國第四個直轄市，轄15個區，25個縣（市）。區域面積82400平方公裏，人口3060萬，是目前中國行政轄區最大的城市。

重慶，是中國歷史文化名城，迄今已有3000多年的歷史，文化源遠流長；

重慶，是世界反法西斯戰爭的前沿陣地，第二次世界大戰的遠東指揮中心；

重慶，擁有以美麗的山水，迷人的夜景，膾炙人口的三國文化遺迹，精美絕倫的大足石刻，雄奇險峻的長江三峽和第二次世界大戰遠東指揮中心遺址爲代表的20多個景區、300多個景點吸引着衆多的海內外游客。

重慶人民大禮堂 Chongqing People's Great Auditorium

Chongqing

Chongqing, a pearl in the upper reaches of Yangtze River, was formally established by China's central government as the nation's fourth directly administered municipality in June, 1997. Chongqing now administers a sprawling area of 82,400 square kilometers that includes 25 counties and cities, 15 districts and a total population exceeding 30,600,000 people.

The city's origins date back over 3,000 years ago, and it is a well known historical and cultural city. Also, it served as China's war-time capital during the Second World War .

Chongqing, a picturesque mountain city, is famous for its fantastic night views, popular cultural relics of the Three Kingdoms, exquisite Duzu Stone Carving, and the attractive Yangtze Three Gorges. They attract more and more tourists from home and abroad.

白鶴梁

　　白鶴梁距涪陵城上游1公裏，江中有一塊巨大的天然石梁，長約1600米，寬約15米。在枯水期，長江水位降到一定程度時，巨大的石梁就會露出江面，好似一衹巨大的白色仙鶴，故稱"白鶴梁"。石梁上有100多幅題刻，記錄了唐代以來長江枯水的珍貴始料。白鶴梁被稱爲"長江古代水文站，白鶴梁是三峽庫區惟一將要被淹沒的國家級文物保護單位。

White-Crane Rock Ridge

　　The White Crane Rock Ridge is one kilometer from the Fuling city. There is a huge natural long rock with an approximate length of 1,600m and width of 15m in the river. In the dry season, when the water level falls down by some degree, the whole rock ridge can be seen, looking like a giant white crane, hence, it is named as the white Crane Rock. On it more than 100 inscriptions and carvings illustrate the valuable historical records about the Yangtze River's low water level since the Tang Dynasty. Also, it receives its nickname as the Yangtze Ancient Hydrometric Station. It is the only state cultural relic protected in the Three Gorges area.

涪陵白鶴梁
Fuling White-Crane Rock Ridge

龍床石 dragon-like bed rock

石魚 rock fish

魅力巫山

豐都鬼城

豐都，被稱爲鬼國京都。由國家級風景名勝古迹豐都名山，全國最大的民俗文化動態人文景觀鬼國神宮和國家級森林公園雙桂山組成。景區林茂竹修，鳥語花香，建築古色古香，雕塑工藝精湛。自漢唐以來，名山逐漸被傳爲鬼國京都，雖閻王小鬼、判官地獄之傳說虛妄，但其懲惡揚善的思想又被人們稱道，成爲集儒、道、佛文化爲一體的民俗文化藝術寶庫。

Fengdu Ghost Town

Fengdu, named as the "Ghost City", is composed of the state tourist attracition Mt.Minshan, the largest man-made folk custom "Ghost City Palace" in China and the national forest park Mt. Shuangguishan. Inside, lush green bamboos, wild flowers and birds, typical Chinese style architecture can be enjoyed. It received its reputation as the "Ghost City" in the Eastern Han Dynasty. The social structure in the hell is exactly like that in the real world. It is the folk custom and art treasures together with Confucianism, Daoism and Buddhaism.

豐都名山 Mt. Mingshan in Fengdu

石寶寨

石寶寨被譽爲江上明珠，是世界八大奇异建築之一。位于重慶忠縣境內長江北岸一個古樸的鄉村小鎮，距忠縣古城38公裏。石寶寨臨江高聳，孤峰拔地，四壁如削，形如玉印，又名玉印山。相傳此山乃女媧煉石補天遺留下來的一塊鎮妖的五彩石，故稱"石寶"；明朝末年，農民起義軍在此安營扎寨，抗擊清兵達三個月之久，石寶寨由此得名。

ShiBaoZhai

ShiBaoZhai represents one of the gems of Chinese architecture along the banks of the Yangtze River. From afar, the hill on the northern bank can appear to resemble a jade seal, and is so named. The creation of the hill is attributed to the goddess Nuwo, who caused a rockslide while she was redecorating the sky after a fierce battle between two warring dukes. The rising waters of the river will eventually surround the pagoda, which will be preserved with a tiny dam of its own, but left on island.

石寶寨 Shibao Stockade

張飛廟

　　"巴蜀一勝景，文藻一勝地"的張飛廟，江上風清，亭閣飛檐，層樓峭拔，煞是壯觀！1980年被列爲四川省第一批重點文物保護單位。它與雲陽縣城隔江相望，始建于1700年前，歷經滄桑，勝而不衰。

Zhangfei Temple

　　The Temple of ZhangFei was built on the opposite of Yunyang County seat in memory of Zhang Fei, the famous General in Shu Kingdom (the three kingdoms' period 220-265). with the statue of Zhang Fei and other cultural relics in the temple. It is listed as the first key cultural relics protection site.

張飛廟 Zhang Fei Temple

白帝城

　　白帝城，位于長江北岸的瞿塘峽口，自古有"詩城"之稱。白帝城原名紫陽城，它是新莽時公孫述割據四川之際建築的。因爲傳說城中有井，井中白霧騰空，其形狀宛如一條白龍，直衝九霄，于是公孫述自稱白帝，城也改爲白帝城。公孫述被東漢光武帝劉秀消滅後，後人便在這裏修了一座白帝廟。白帝城因三國故事"劉備托孤"而廣泛流傳，一直名聞中外。三峽工程蓄水後，水將淹至半山腰，形成水霧繚繞、仙山群閣般的勝景。

White King Town

　　The White King Town, named as "Poem City", is located at the entrance of Qutang Gorge. Towards the end of the Western Han Dyansty, Gong Sunshu built a walled town on the mountain before he occupied Shu Kingdom, the present-day Sichuan Province. Also, as a well in the town often gave off white steam shaped like a white dragon, Gong Sunshu called himself White King and named the town White King Town so as to match the White Dragon. The White King Town is pretty popular because of a story that happened in the Three kingdom period. It was Liu Bei, the king of Shu, entrusted his son to his prime minister. With the completion of the dam, the water will reach halfway of the mountain, forming a misty and fairy island.

白帝廟 White King Temple

屈原祠

　　屈原祠坐落于古城歸洲鎮。
　　屈原祠是爲紀念屈原而修建的，屈原，名平。公元前340年誕生于秭歸縣樂平裏，是我國最早的偉大愛國詩人。他曾在古代楚國做過和三閭大夫，後因奸臣排擠放逐江南，當楚國被秦兵攻破時，他憤而以身殉國，投汨羅江而死。其《離騷》、《九章》、《九歌》等詩篇，聲貫古今，名揚中外，1935年聯合國教科文組織將屈原列爲世界文化名人。

Qu Yuan Shrine

　　The Qu Yuan Shrine is located in the ancient GuizhouTown..
　　The Qu Yuan Shrine was built to memorize Qu Yuan. Qu Yuan, also named ping, the earliest patriotic poet in China, was born in 340 B.C. in Lepingli of Zigui County. He once Served as a supervisor and imperial household administrator in the ancient Chu State. Then squeezed by malicious minister, he was expelled to a place south of the Yangtze River. When the army of the Qing State captured the Chu, he was so overcome with indignation and sorrow that he jumped into the Miluo River. His poems and articles including Laments at parting, Nine Lyrical Poems and Nine Sacrificial Songs are well known all over the world. in 1953, Qu Yuan is listed to one of the cultural famous men in the world by UNESCO.

1.屈原祠 Quyuan Temple
2.屈原銅像 Quyuan Bronze Statue
3.昭君像 Zhao Jun Statue
4.昭君故裏 birthplace of Zhao Jun

昭君故裏

　　"群山萬壑赴荆門，生長明妃尚有村"。杜甫詩中所說的明妃村位于湖北省興山縣香溪河畔的寶村，歷代相傳是我國民族和睦使者和古代四大美女之一王昭君的故鄉。

　　三峽工程蓄水139米水位後，對昭君故裏的控訪不僅沒有影響，反而便利了許多，游客乘船從西陵峽西口處的香溪河口進入，直抵興山縣峽口鎮碼頭，再驅車近10公裏便可到達。

Wang Zhaojun's Hometown

　　The poet Du Fu once worte these linese, "Having scaled mountain after mountain on the way to Jingmen, you find the village where the village where the Illustrious Imperial Concubine was born." The village referred to above is located at Baoping Village beside the Xiangxi River in Xingshan County, Hubei Province. According to legend, the village is the hometown of Wang Zhaojun-an envoy for national peace and also one of the four top beauties in ancient China.

　　After the reservoir water lever rose to 139 meters, to visit Wang Zhaojun's hometown isn't affected. Instead, it is more convenient than before. You can take a ship from the mouth of the Xiangxi River at the west mouth of the Xiling Gorge, directly to the dork of Xiakou Town in Xingshan County. Then it will take only a 10 kilometer's drive to get there .

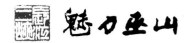

長江三峽水利樞紐

長江三峽工程壩址位于宜昌市三鬥坪中堡島，是當今世界上最大的水利樞紐工程。三峽工程采用"一級開發，一次建成，分期蓄水，連續移民"的方案。工程總工期17年，分三個階段施工：第一階段1993-1997年，爲施工準備階段及一期工程；第二階段1998-2003年，爲二期工程；第三階段2004-2009年，爲三期工程。水庫最終淹沒耕地43.13萬畝，最終將移民113.18萬人。工程竣工後，水庫正常蓄水175米，防洪庫容221.5億立方米，總庫容達393億立方米，可充分發揮其在長江中下游防洪體系中的關鍵性骨幹作用，并將顯著改善宜昌致重慶660公裏的航道，萬噸級船隊可直達重慶港，將發揮防洪、發電、航運、養殖、旅游、保護生態、淨化環境、開發性移民、南水北調、防洪灌慨等十大效益，是目前世界上任何巨型電站無法比擬的！

三峽大壩 Yangtze Three Gorge Dam

The Yangtze Three Gorges Project

The Three Gorges Dam, the largest water conservancy project ever undertaken by man, is now being built in Sandouping area of Yichang City. The project will be built by the guideline of "continuous development and construction of the super structure, impoundment in different stages and phases of resettlement". The total time for the project is 17 years. It will be divided into three stages. The first stage is from 1993 to1997, the second stage is from 1998 to 2003, and the third is from 2004 to 2009. More than 430, 000 acres of farmland will be flooded, causing 1.3 million people to be relocated. Finally the dam will raise the river to a level of 175 meters above sea level, creating a reservoir with flood control capacity of 22.1 billion cubic meters and a storage capacity of 39.9 billion cubic meters. The builling of the huge dam is for the purpose of flood control, electricity genenation, navigation, environmental purification, redevelopmental resettlement and transferring water from the South to North. After the dam is built, it can improve the flood control capacity of the middle and lower regions of the Yangtze River. It will increase the shipping capacity from the dam site all the way to Chongqing 660 km away. All these make it a unique project in the world!

長江三峽水利樞紐工程
Yangtze Three Gorges water conservency project

泄洪 Flood Discharge

魅力巫山

大昌古鎮
Ancient Dachang Town

小小三峽
Mini Three Gorges

▲ 梨子坪國家森林公園

大昌湖

雙鷹戲屏
Two eagles playing on sereen

飛雲洞

船棺

蟒蛇飲水

登天峰

羅家寨

▲ 平河度假村

懸棺

大

群仙迎賓

巴霧峽
Misty G

雙龍鎮
Shuanglong Town ○

寧

懸棺
The Cliff Coffin

蓬莟峰
The buddha's peak

八戒拜觀音

仙桃峰

河

民俗文化村

桂花移民新村
東坪湖

龍

熊貓飲水

青獅衛門

靈芝峰

奉節縣
Fengjie County

白帝城
White King Town

巫山縣
Wushan County

大寧湖
Daning Lake

重慶
Chongqing
◎

豐都鬼城
Fengdu
Ghost Town

石寶寨
ShiBao Zhai

張飛廟
ZhangFei Temple

神女峰
Goddess peak

集仙峰
The Jixian

白鶴梁
White-Crane Rock Ridge

長

青石
Qingshi

江

神
女
溪

Shennu Stream

瞿塘峽 Qutang Gorge

巫峽 Wu Gorge

巫山旅游景點分布圖
Tourist Sketch Map of the Wushan

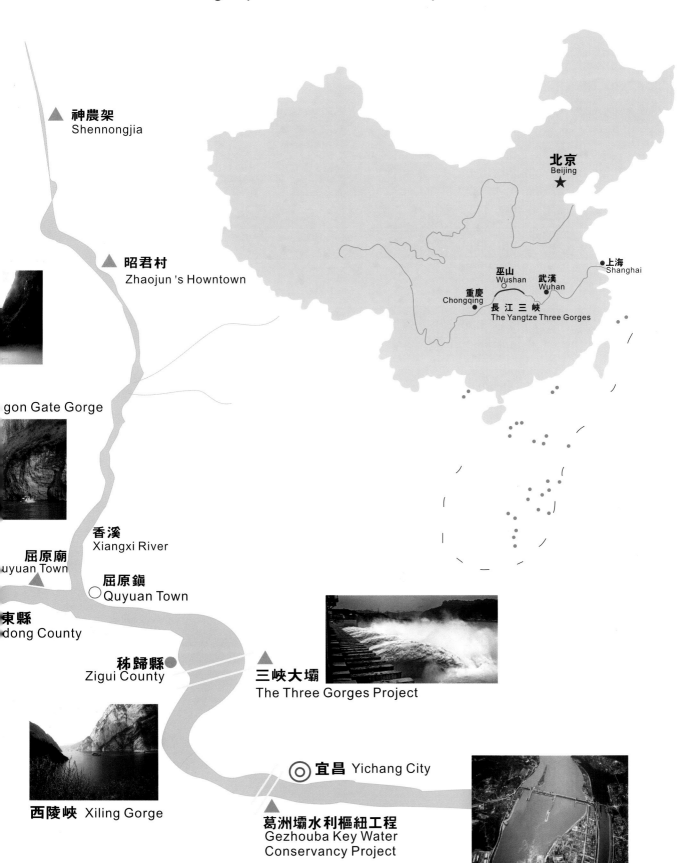

巫山在中國的地理位置
Geographical Position Map of the Wushan in China

神農架
Shennongjia

昭君村
Zhaojun 's Howntown

北京
Beijing
★

上海
Shanghai

巫山
Wushan

重慶
Chongqing

武漢
Wuhan

長 江 三 峽
The Yangtze Three Gorges

gon Gate Gorge

香溪
Xiangxi River

屈原廟
uyuan Town

屈原鎮
Quyuan Town

東縣
dong County

秭歸縣
Zigui County

三峽大壩
The Three Gorges Project

宜昌 Yichang City

西陵峽 Xiling Gorge

葛洲壩水利樞紐工程
Gezhouba Key Water
Conservancy Project

124

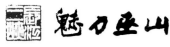

後 記 | Postscript

Postscript

　　宋开平，重庆市巫山县人，中国摄影家协会会员，重庆市摄影家协会理事，重庆市巫山县摄影协会主席。

　　我生在三峡、長在三峡、工作在三峡、退休在三峡，一個土生土長的三峡人。從孩提時代到人生暮年，我親眼見證了三峡的滄海桑田、歲月變遷，也親手記錄了三峡的一草一木、一山一水。是三峡這片熱土培育了我，是勤勞樸實的三峡人民乳汁養育了我。數十年的攝影創作，讓我與三峡的山、三峡的水、三峡的雲、三峡的人結下了深深的不解之緣，也積累了數以萬計的攝影作品。

　　多年來，我一直希望能把自己所看到的、感受到的、領悟到的三峡告訴給更多的人，讓更多的人們知道三峡、認識三峡、了解三峡、熱愛三峡，走進三峡，也為宣傳家鄉盡一份心，獻一份力。于是，我想到應再編寫一本以巫山風光為主體，全面介紹長江三峡的綜合性畫冊，回報家鄉父老。編輯這本冊子，它應該集藝術性、資料性、收藏性為一體，多角度、高層次地展示三峡的壯美風光、風土民情、歷史文化和滄桑巨變，通過自己的攝影語言，把自己對三峡的一些膚淺認識傳遞給讀者，這便是編寫這本《魅力巫山》的初衷。

　　在本書策劃過程中，得到了重慶揚子江國旅、宜昌思源影視文化傳媒有限公司及盧進、江上、健康、培清等影友的鼎力相助，在此一一致謝！

作 者

2007年7月

　　Song kaiping, born in Wushan County, is Chairman of Wushan Photography Association, Director of Chongqing Photography Association, and member of China Photography Association.

　　I am a typical native Three Gorges man, born, raised, worked, and retired in the Three Gorges.I have witnessed great changes in the Three Gorges during my life. Every blade of grass, every tree, every mountain, and every river in my hometown has been recorded in my pictures. The Three Gorges have raised me, the honest and industrious Three Gorges people have brought me up.After dozens of years of picture taking, it seems to me that I can not live without the mountains, rivers, clouds and people in the Three Gorges area. This is why I have a great collection of the Three gorges photographs.

　　In recent years, in order to let more and more people know, learn, understand, love and explore the three gorges, I would like to publicize my hometown through my pictures and to share my own experience with you. To thank my lovely hometown, I would like to publish a comprehensive picture book, focusing on the beautiful scenery of Wushan as well as the Yangtze Three Gorges. This book would also feature its art, information and give a complete record of the Three Gorges. The purpose of this book is to let all the readers learn and know more about the Three Gorges' attractive sceneries, folk customs, culture, history and great changes.

　　I am very grateful to the following with great help for this book. The Chongqing Yangtze International Travel Service, the Yichang Siyuan Video Culture media Co. Ltd, together with my photograph pals, Chu Qing, Lu Jin, Jiang Shang, Jing kang and Pei Qing.

图书在版编目 (CIP) 数据

长江三峡经典摄影：汉、英对照/卢进、宋开平摄.-海口：海南出版社，
2008.2
ISBN 978-7-80564-973-3

Ⅰ. 长...　Ⅱ. 卢...　Ⅲ. ①风光摄影-中国-现代-摄影
集②三峡-摄影集　Ⅳ.J424

中国版本图书馆CIP数据核字(2008)第016115号

长江三峡经典摄影 魅力巫山 （汉、英对照）

作　者：宋开平		责任编辑：万　胜	
出版策划：卢　进		翻　译：George Zhao 赵培清	
装帧设计：朱红霞　狄德华			
出　版：海南出版社		邮　编：570216	
地　址：海口市金盘开发区建设三横路2号			
发　行：全国新华书店经销			
制作印刷：深圳市精典印务有限公司			
开　本：16开		印　张：8	
版　次：2011年2月第2版　2011年2月第2次印刷			
书　号：ISBN 978-7-80564-973-3			
定　价：158元			